MAD LIBS®

FIRST DAY OF SCHOOL
MAD LIBS

by Kim Ostrow

MAD LIBS
An Imprint of Penguin Random House LLC, New York

Mad Libs format and text copyright © 2021 by Penguin Random House LLC.
All rights reserved.

Concept created by Roger Price & Leonard Stern

Cover illustration by Scott Brooks

Published by Mad Libs,
an imprint of Penguin Random House LLC, New York.
Printed in the USA.

Visit us online at www.penguinrandomhouse.com.

ISBN 9780593225875
1 3 5 7 9 10 8 6 4 2

MAD LIBS

INSTRUCTIONS

MAD LIBS® is a game for people who don't like games! It can be played by one, two, three, four, or forty.

● RIDICULOUSLY SIMPLE DIRECTIONS

In this tablet you will find stories containing blank spaces where words are left out. One player, the READER, selects one of these stories. The READER does not tell anyone what the story is about. Instead, he/she asks the other players, the WRITERS, to give him/her words. These words are used to fill in the blank spaces in the story.

● TO PLAY

The READER asks each WRITER in turn to call out a word—an adjective or a noun or whatever the space calls for—and uses them to fill in the blank spaces in the story. The result is a MAD LIBS® game.

When the READER then reads the completed MAD LIBS® game to the other players, they will discover that they have written a story that is fantastic, screamingly funny, shocking, silly, crazy, or just plain dumb—depending upon which words each WRITER called out.

● EXAMPLE (*Before* and *After*)

"_____!" he said _____
         EXCLAMATION   ADVERB

as he jumped into his convertible _____ and
                                              NOUN

drove off with his _____ wife.
                          ADJECTIVE

"_____OUCH_____!" he said _____HAPPILY_____
         EXCLAMATION   ADVERB

as he jumped into his convertible _____CAT_____ and
                                              NOUN

drove off with his _____BRAVE_____ wife.
                          ADJECTIVE

QUICK REVIEW

In case you have forgotten what adjectives, adverbs, nouns, and verbs are, here is a quick review:

An ADJECTIVE describes something or somebody. *Lumpy*, *soft*, *ugly*, *messy*, and *short* are adjectives.

An ADVERB tells how something is done. It modifies a verb and usually ends in "ly." *Modestly*, *stupidly*, *greedily*, and *carefully* are adverbs.

A NOUN is the name of a person, place, or thing. *Sidewalk*, *umbrella*, *bridle*, *bathtub*, and *nose* are nouns.

A VERB is an action word. *Run*, *pitch*, *jump*, and *swim* are verbs. Put the verbs in past tense if the directions say PAST TENSE. *Ran*, *pitched*, *jumped*, and *swam* are verbs in the past tense.

When we ask for A PLACE, we mean any sort of place: a country or city (*Spain*, *Cleveland*) or a room (*bathroom*, *kitchen*).

An EXCLAMATION or SILLY WORD is any sort of funny sound, gasp, grunt, or outcry, like *Wow!*, *Ouch!*, *Whomp!*, *Ick!*, and *Gadzooks!*

When we ask for specific words, like a NUMBER, a COLOR, an ANIMAL, or a PART OF THE BODY, we mean a word that is one of those things, like *seven*, *blue*, *horse*, or *head*.

When we ask for a PLURAL, it means more than one. For example, *cat* pluralized is *cats*.

MAD LIBS® is fun to play with friends, but you can also play it by yourself! To begin with, DO NOT look at the story on the page below. Fill in the blanks on this page with the words called for. Then, using the words you have selected, fill in the blank spaces in the story.

Now you've created your own hilarious MAD LIBS® game!

WELCOME BACK!

CELEBRITY _____

ADJECTIVE _____

VERB ENDING IN "ING" _____

PLURAL NOUN _____

COUNTRY _____

VERB ENDING IN "ING" _____

TYPE OF BUILDING _____

TYPE OF FOOD _____

ANIMAL _____

PERSON IN ROOM _____

PART OF THE BODY _____

TYPE OF CONTAINER _____

SILLY WORD _____

NUMBER _____

COLOR _____

NOUN _____

VERB ENDING IN "ING" _____

ADJECTIVE _____

MAD LIBS®

WELCOME BACK!

Good morning, students! As your principal, I am pleased to welcome

you back to _____ Middle School. It is _____
      CELEBRITY   ADJECTIVE

to see all your _____ faces. I hope you had a great
               VERB ENDING IN "ING"

summer and got to spend time with your _____ or visit
                                   PLURAL NOUN

somewhere fancy like the Eiffel Tower in _____. My
                                     COUNTRY

family and I went on a/an _____ trip. We slept
                     VERB ENDING IN "ING"

in a canvas _____ and cooked _____
         TYPE OF BUILDING   TYPE OF FOOD

over an open fire. One night, the local grizzly _____,
                                  ANIMAL

affectionately referred to as Cutie _____, got his
                         PERSON IN ROOM

_____ caught in our picnic _____.
  PART OF THE BODY   TYPE OF CONTAINER

He caused quite a/an _____ that evening, and we *bearly*
                 SILLY WORD

made it out of our campsite! But enough about me! The next

_____ days are all about you. The _____-boards
   NUMBER   COLOR

are as clean as a/an _____, and your teachers have been
                    NOUN

_____ hard to prepare for your first day of school!
 VERB ENDING IN "ING"

Let's have a/an _____ year!
           ADJECTIVE

From FIRST DAY OF SCHOOL MAD LIBS® • Copyright © 2021 by Penguin Random House LLC.

MAD LIBS® is fun to play with friends, but you can also play it by yourself! To begin with, DO NOT look at the story on the page below. Fill in the blanks on this page with the words called for. Then, using the words you have selected, fill in the blank spaces in the story.

Now you've created your own hilarious MAD LIBS® game!

IN YOUR DREAMS

ADJECTIVE _____

ARTICLE OF CLOTHING _____

PART OF THE BODY _____

TYPE OF LIQUID _____

ADJECTIVE _____

CELEBRITY _____

NOUN _____

TYPE OF FOOD _____

ANIMAL _____

VERB _____

VEHICLE _____

SILLY WORD _____

NOUN _____

ADVERB _____

NOUN _____

ADJECTIVE _____

NOUN _____

EXCLAMATION _____

MAD LIBS®

IN YOUR DREAMS

Everyone has _____ dreams before the first day of school!
                   ADJECTIVE

Last night, I dreamed that I woke up for school and put on a clown's

_____. Then, I rinsed out my _____
ARTICLE OF CLOTHING   PART OF THE BODY

with mouth-_____ and went downstairs for breakfast.
              TYPE OF LIQUID

That's when my dream got even more _____. _____
                                          ADJECTIVE   CELEBRITY

was sitting at my kitchen _____ eating a bowl of
                                  NOUN

_____. After that, my brother reminded me to bring my pet
TYPE OF FOOD

_____ to school for _____ and Tell. When the
     ANIMAL   VERB

school _____ pulled up outside, I shouted, "_____!"
         VEHICLE   SILLY WORD

and ran outside to get a seat. I'm glad I put on my _____-belt,
                                                           NOUN

because then the bus driver _____ deployed a pair of
                                    ADVERB

_____-powered jet engines and the bus started flying!
     NOUN

Suddenly, I heard a/an _____ noise that got louder and
                            ADJECTIVE

louder. That's when I finally woke up. The noise was my alarm

_____ waking me up for my first day! Anyway, I guess the
     NOUN

good thing about having weird dreams the night before school is that

it makes *actually* going to school so much easier! _____!
                                                          EXCLAMATION

MAD LIBS® is fun to play with friends, but you can also play it by yourself! To begin with, DO NOT look at the story on the page below. Fill in the blanks on this page with the words called for. Then, using the words you have selected, fill in the blank spaces in the story.

Now you've created your own hilarious MAD LIBS® game!

ALL ABOARD!

ADJECTIVE _____

NUMBER _____

TYPE OF BUILDING _____

TYPE OF FOOD _____

PLURAL NOUN _____

VERB _____

ADJECTIVE _____

VERB ENDING IN "ING" _____

VERB _____

ANIMAL _____

ADJECTIVE _____

NOUN _____

OCCUPATION _____

PLURAL NOUN _____

MAD LIBS

ALL ABOARD!

There are a lot of _____ ways to get to school. Here's a list
                        ADJECTIVE

of the top _____ :
            NUMBER

1. **The _____ bus:** Watch out for _____ stuck
         TYPE OF BUILDING   TYPE OF FOOD

   under the seats and hold onto your hardcover _____ in
                                                 PLURAL NOUN

   case the driver has to _____ the brakes.
                           VERB

2. **Bicycle:** Check the weather, because it's _____ to hold
                                                 ADJECTIVE

   an umbrella while _____ .
                      VERB ENDING IN "ING"

3. **Walk:** Don't stop to _____ every _____ along
                            VERB   ANIMAL

   the way or you'll be _____ for school!
                         ADJECTIVE

4. **Skate-_____ :** Cool, but if the _____ catches
           NOUN   OCCUPATION

   you doing jumps off the school's front _____ , you're
                                           PLURAL NOUN

   getting detention!

From FIRST DAY OF SCHOOL MAD LIBS® • Copyright © 2021 by Penguin Random House LLC.

MAD LIBS® is fun to play with friends, but you can also play it by yourself! To begin with, DO NOT look at the story on the page below. Fill in the blanks on this page with the words called for. Then, using the words you have selected, fill in the blank spaces in the story.

Now you've created your own hilarious MAD LIBS® game!

WHAT TO WEAR WHERE

ADJECTIVE _____

ARTICLE OF CLOTHING _____

COLOR _____

PLURAL NOUN _____

PERSON IN ROOM _____

VERB ENDING IN "ING" _____

CELEBRITY _____

VERB _____

ADVERB _____

SOMETHING ALIVE (PLURAL) _____

NUMBER _____

ARTICLE OF CLOTHING (PLURAL) _____

ADVERB _____

ADJECTIVE _____

OCCUPATION _____

VERB _____

NOUN _____

PLURAL NOUN _____

MAD LIBS®

WHAT TO WEAR WHERE

Getting dressed for the first day of school is so _____!
ADJECTIVE

I'm going to wear my favorite wool _____. It's
ARTICLE OF CLOTHING

_____ and has _____ all over it. I bought it last
COLOR   PLURAL NOUN

year at my favorite store: _____'s Vintage Sweater Shoppe.
PERSON IN ROOM

I was out _____ with my friend _____
VERB ENDING IN "ING"   CELEBRITY

when I saw it in the window and I just had to _____ it.
VERB

_____, I had saved up enough money from babysitting
ADVERB

my neighbor's _____. Plus, it was on sale for
SOMETHING ALIVE (PLURAL)

_____ percent off! This sweater is going to match my
NUMBER

_____ _____. To complete the look,
ARTICLE OF CLOTHING (PLURAL)   ADVERB

I'm going to wear the _____ jeans my _____
ADJECTIVE   OCCUPATION

grew out of. She gave them to me, and they _____ like a/an
VERB

_____. My outfit is set! And the best part is, I'm gonna look
NOUN

like a million _____ on the first day of school, even though
PLURAL NOUN

I barely spent any money at all!

MAD LIBS® is fun to play with friends, but you can also play it by yourself! To begin with, DO NOT look at the story on the page below. Fill in the blanks on this page with the words called for. Then, using the words you have selected, fill in the blank spaces in the story.

Now you've created your own hilarious MAD LIBS® game!

CLASS RULES

VERB _____

PLURAL NOUN _____

ADJECTIVE _____

PART OF THE BODY _____

SOMETHING ALIVE (PLURAL) _____

PLURAL NOUN _____

NOUN _____

TYPE OF FOOD _____

NOUN _____

ADJECTIVE _____

PART OF THE BODY (PLURAL) _____

VERB _____

PLURAL NOUN _____

OCCUPATION _____

VERB _____

ADJECTIVE _____

MAD LIBS®

CLASS RULES

1. **Be polite:** Do not _____ while the teacher is talking.

VERB

   Be respectful of classmates and _____ by using

PLURAL NOUN

   _____ language, raising your _____ , and

ADJECTIVE   PART OF THE BODY

   listening to your fellow _____ . No cellular

SOMETHING ALIVE (PLURAL)

   _____ in class.

PLURAL NOUN

2. **Be prepared:** Always bring a/an _____ to class. Do not

NOUN

   chew _____ in class. If you are hungry, please wait for

TYPE OF FOOD

   _____ time.

NOUN

3. **Be _____ :** Keep your _____ on your

ADJECTIVE   PART OF THE BODY (PLURAL)

   own work and _____ in your seat during tests.

VERB

4. **Be clean:** Put away your _____ . (Your teacher is not

PLURAL NOUN

   your _____ .)

OCCUPATION

5. _____ **hard** and have a/an _____ year!

VERB   ADJECTIVE

MAD LIBS® is fun to play with friends, but you can also play it by yourself! To begin with, DO NOT look at the story on the page below. Fill in the blanks on this page with the words called for. Then, using the words you have selected, fill in the blank spaces in the story.

Now you've created your own hilarious MAD LIBS® game!

REPORT ON WHAT I DID LAST SUMMER

VERB ENDING IN "ING" _____

ADJECTIVE _____

VERB _____

PLURAL NOUN _____

VERB _____

ADJECTIVE _____

SILLY WORD _____

ADJECTIVE _____

PLURAL NOUN _____

VERB _____

VERB (PAST TENSE) _____

TYPE OF FOOD _____

NUMBER _____

ANIMAL _____

ADJECTIVE _____

EXCLAMATION _____

VERB _____

MAD LIBS
REPORT ON WHAT I DID LAST SUMMER

This summer, my parents didn't want me _____

<u>VERB ENDING IN "ING"</u>

around all day complaining that I was _____, so they signed

<u>ADJECTIVE</u>

me up for camp. But I couldn't decide which one to _____.

<u>VERB</u>

Did you know that there are sports camps, _____ camps,

<u>PLURAL NOUN</u>

and even camps where you learn to sing and _____? It was

<u>VERB</u>

a/an _____ decision. We settled on a place called Camp

<u>ADJECTIVE</u>

_____ Lake, and it was _____! We slept in these

<u>SILLY WORD</u>   <u>ADJECTIVE</u>

cabins made of _____, with no electricity. At night, it got

<u>PLURAL NOUN</u>

pretty dark, so we used our flashlights to _____. During

<u>VERB</u>

the day, we went swimming and _____ on the

<u>VERB (PAST TENSE)</u>

trampoline. The best part was the food, especially the peanut butter

and _____ sandwiches. And I only got _____

<u>TYPE OF FOOD</u>   <u>NUMBER</u>

_____ bites, which I thought was pretty lucky. When camp

<u>ANIMAL</u>

ended, I was so _____. It was hard to say "_____"

<u>ADJECTIVE</u>   <u>EXCLAMATION</u>

to all my new friends. But at least I knew I had this cool story to

_____ about on the first day of school!

<u>VERB</u>

MAD LIBS® is fun to play with friends, but you can also play it by yourself! To begin with, DO NOT look at the story on the page below. Fill in the blanks on this page with the words called for. Then, using the words you have selected, fill in the blank spaces in the story.

Now you've created your own hilarious MAD LIBS® game!

SCHOOL SUPPLIES

ADJECTIVE _____

NUMBER _____

PLURAL NOUN _____

COLOR _____

ADJECTIVE _____

TYPE OF CONTAINER _____

NUMBER _____

NOUN _____

VERB _____

PLURAL NOUN _____

NOUN _____

PART OF THE BODY _____

NOUN _____

PLURAL NOUN _____

TYPE OF LIQUID _____

VERB _____

SILLY WORD _____

It's _____ to start the year with lots of school supplies.
      ADJECTIVE

You'll need:

1. Twenty Number _____ pencils and twenty ballpoint
             NUMBER

   _____ (with blue or _____ ink). Don't forget
   PLURAL NOUN   COLOR

   your _____ pencil _____.
     ADJECTIVE   TYPE OF CONTAINER

2. A/An _____ -ring binder with _____ dividers.
      NUMBER   NOUN

   I _____ staying organized.
    VERB

3. Four single-subject note-_____
            PLURAL NOUN

4. Glue stick and scissors for _____ class. Did you know
            NOUN

   they make special scissors for people who cut with their left

   _____?
  PART OF THE BODY

5. A solar-powered _____. I like calculators with a lot of
           NOUN

   _____ to press.
   PLURAL NOUN

6. A/An _____ bottle
    TYPE OF LIQUID

7. Tissues . . . because you never know when you're going to

   _____ in class. _____!
    VERB   SILLY WORD

MAD LIBS® is fun to play with friends, but you can also play it by yourself! To begin with, DO NOT look at the story on the page below. Fill in the blanks on this page with the words called for. Then, using the words you have selected, fill in the blank spaces in the story.

Now you've created your own hilarious MAD LIBS® game!

FIELD TRIP
PERMISSION FORM

OCCUPATION _____

TYPE OF BUILDING _____

PLURAL NOUN _____

PERSON IN ROOM _____

ADJECTIVE _____

ADJECTIVE _____

SOMETHING ALIVE _____

FIRST NAME _____

LAST NAME _____

ADJECTIVE _____

TYPE OF FOOD _____

VEHICLE _____

NOUN _____

NOUN _____

ANIMAL _____

NUMBER _____

LETTER OF THE ALPHABET _____

CELEBRITY _____

MAD LIBS®
FIELD TRIP
PERMISSION FORM

Dear Parent or _____ ,
OCCUPATION

Your child's class will be going on a field trip to the _____
TYPE OF BUILDING

of Natural History to learn about _____ . As always, we expect
PLURAL NOUN

_____ to be on their _____ behavior when not
PERSON IN ROOM   ADJECTIVE

on school grounds. _____ conduct will result in detention.
ADJECTIVE

If you agree to allow your _____ to attend, please
SOMETHING ALIVE

complete the form below:

I, _____ _____ give permission for my child to go
FIRST NAME   LAST NAME

to the Museum of _____ History. I understand that
ADJECTIVE

transportation and _____ will be provided, and that my child
TYPE OF FOOD

will be traveling by _____ . During the _____ trip, I
VEHICLE   NOUN

can be reached on my _____ , or you can contact me by email
NOUN

at _____-_____ @ _____ -mail.com.
ANIMAL   NUMBER   LETTER OF THE ALPHABET

In case of emergency, please contact _____ .
CELEBRITY

MAD LIBS® is fun to play with friends, but you can also play it by yourself! To begin with, DO NOT look at the story on the page below. Fill in the blanks on this page with the words called for. Then, using the words you have selected, fill in the blank spaces in the story.

Now you've created your own hilarious MAD LIBS® game!

SUBSTITUTE TEACHER

OCCUPATION _____

ANIMAL _____

PART OF THE BODY _____

NOUN _____

VERB _____

ADJECTIVE _____

SILLY WORD _____

VERB ENDING IN "ING" _____

EXCLAMATION _____

ADVERB _____

NOUN _____

VERB _____

VERB ENDING IN "ING" _____

ADJECTIVE _____

NUMBER _____

ADJECTIVE _____

NOUN _____

MAD LIBS®

SUBSTITUTE TEACHER

Today in math, we had a very unusual substitute _____.
OCCUPATION

Our regular teacher, Mr. _____, was out sick with a/an
ANIMAL

_____ cold. The entire class had really low _____,
PART OF THE BODY   NOUN

so the substitute made us _____ around the room to wake
VERB

up. Things got a little more _____ when the substitute made
ADJECTIVE

us cheer "_____" at the top of our lungs over and over.
SILLY WORD

"Keep _____!" he said. Then, he got us all to stand in
VERB ENDING IN "ING"

a single-file line. "_____! March like you're in a parade,"
EXCLAMATION

he said _____. He even suggested we pick up a/an
ADVERB

_____ from our desk and _____ it around in the
NOUN   VERB

air like a baton. The whole class ended up _____
VERB ENDING IN "ING"

around our desks. At first it felt weird, but it was actually really

_____! I didn't even mind that he gave us _____
ADJECTIVE   NUMBER

hours of homework. I hope our regular teacher gets _____
ADJECTIVE

soon, but maybe just a few more days tucked in his _____
NOUN

at home would be for the best!

MAD LIBS® is fun to play with friends, but you can also play it by yourself! To begin with, DO NOT look at the story on the page below. Fill in the blanks on this page with the words called for. Then, using the words you have selected, fill in the blank spaces in the story.

Now you've created your own hilarious MAD LIBS® game!

BACK TO SCHOOL POEM

ADJECTIVE _____

VERB _____

NOUN _____

VERB ENDING IN "ING" _____

ADVERB _____

PLURAL NOUN _____

OCCUPATION _____

NOUN _____

PLURAL NOUN _____

PERSON IN ROOM _____

TYPE OF LIQUID _____

VERB _____

OCCUPATION _____

NOUN _____

VERB _____

PLURAL NOUN _____

MAD LIBS®

BACK TO SCHOOL POEM

When the _____ summer ends,
ADJECTIVE

it's time to _____ at school with all my friends.
VERB

I love the first _____ of school
NOUN

because _____ is so cool.
VERB ENDING IN "ING"

I _____ walk up the _____ (and never run),
ADVERB   PLURAL NOUN

so the hall _____ doesn't ruin my fun.
OCCUPATION

Studying _____ and _____ are great,
NOUN   PLURAL NOUN

but science is better—

except when _____ spilled _____ on my sweater.
PERSON IN ROOM   TYPE OF LIQUID

But most of all, I really _____ math
VERB

because being a/an _____ is my career path!
OCCUPATION

So, before I get in my _____ each night,
NOUN

I _____ my clock,
VERB

knowing tomorrow's _____ are going to rock!
PLURAL NOUN

MAD LIBS® is fun to play with friends, but you can also play it by yourself! To begin with, DO NOT look at the story on the page below. Fill in the blanks on this page with the words called for. Then, using the words you have selected, fill in the blank spaces in the story.

Now you've created your own hilarious MAD LIBS® game!

LIBRARY VISIT

VERB _____

ADJECTIVE _____

SILLY WORD _____

NOUN _____

PART OF THE BODY _____

ADJECTIVE _____

NOUN _____

ANIMAL _____

PLURAL NOUN _____

VERB _____

ADJECTIVE _____

VERB _____

VERB _____

PLURAL NOUN _____

ADVERB _____

VERB ENDING IN "ING" _____

One thing I really _____ about the first day of school is

VERB

our trip to the library—mostly because our school librarian is so

_____! Our librarian's name is Mrs. _____, and she

ADJECTIVE   SILLY WORD

wears _____-rimmed glasses on top of her _____.

NOUN   PART OF THE BODY

She's the most _____ teacher in the entire school. She sits

ADJECTIVE

behind a huge _____ that has a/an _____

NOUN   ANIMAL

tank on it. She knows every _____ on the shelves and

PLURAL NOUN

teaches us to _____ into the computer network so we

VERB

can find the books we want. If you can't find a book that sounds

_____, she will suggest something for you. She'll even

ADJECTIVE

_____ up and down the aisles of the library until she finds

VERB

the book you want to _____. Oh, and she always puts a jar

VERB

of _____ on her desk for the first day of school! Then, if

PLURAL NOUN

you sit _____ in the library, you get a toy! As a result,

ADVERB

it's always quiet in our library. You can almost hear what everyone is

_____!

VERB ENDING IN "ING"

MAD LIBS® is fun to play with friends, but you can also play it by yourself! To begin with, DO NOT look at the story on the page below. Fill in the blanks on this page with the words called for. Then, using the words you have selected, fill in the blank spaces in the story.

Now you've created your own hilarious MAD LIBS® game!

SCIENCE FAIR

TYPE OF EVENT _____

VERB ENDING IN "ING" _____

ADJECTIVE _____

VERB (PAST TENSE) _____

NOUN _____

VERB ENDING IN "ING" _____

ADVERB _____

TYPE OF LIQUID _____

PART OF THE BODY _____

ADJECTIVE _____

VERB _____

PLURAL NOUN _____

TYPE OF FOOD _____

SOMETHING ALIVE (PLURAL) _____

NOUN _____

ADJECTIVE _____

COLOR _____

ANIMAL _____

VERB _____

MAD LIBS®

SCIENCE FAIR

I know it's only the first day of school, but it's never too early to start

planning my _____ project! Last year, I made a/an
                    TYPE OF EVENT

_____ volcano. My favorite part was the _____
VERB ENDING IN "ING"   ADJECTIVE

lava explosion. When the vinegar _____ with the baking
                                   VERB (PAST TENSE)

_____ , it caused a chemical reaction and lava started
       NOUN

_____ out the top. I must have poured too
       VERB ENDING IN "ING"

_____ because the _____ bubbled up
       ADVERB   TYPE OF LIQUID

and splashed all over my _____! This year, I have
                          PART OF THE BODY

something _____ planned. I am going to see how long
             ADJECTIVE

it takes for mold to _____ on different _____ .
                        VERB   PLURAL NOUN

There are so many foods I can use for my experiment: a slice of

_____ , some _____ , or even a hunk
   TYPE OF FOOD   SOMETHING ALIVE (PLURAL)

of raw _____ . The _____ part will be waiting
            NOUN   ADJECTIVE

to see which gets _____ fuzzies on it first. But I think I
                      COLOR

should probably keep the door to my room closed so our family

_____ doesn't try to _____ my experiment!
   ANIMAL   VERB

MAD LIBS® is fun to play with friends, but you can also play it by yourself! To begin with, DO NOT look at the story on the page below. Fill in the blanks on this page with the words called for. Then, using the words you have selected, fill in the blank spaces in the story.

Now you've created your own hilarious MAD LIBS® game!

GYM CLASS

NOUN _____

ADJECTIVE _____

PLURAL NOUN _____

VERB _____

NOUN _____

VERB _____

PLURAL NOUN _____

VERB _____

VERB (PAST TENSE) _____

ADJECTIVE _____

VERB _____

PLURAL NOUN _____

ADVERB _____

NOUN _____

PLURAL NOUN _____

ADVERB _____

ADJECTIVE _____

MAD LIBS®

GYM CLASS

On the first day of gym class, we always play an exciting game of

Capture the _____. The point of the game is quite
                    NOUN

_____ : Be the first team to capture all the _____
ADJECTIVE   PLURAL NOUN

and bring them to your side of the gym. Here's how to _____ :
                                                           VERB

Once the teacher blows the _____ , each team tries to
                                NOUN

_____ the other team's _____ . You have
     VERB   PLURAL NOUN

to be careful not to get caught—if you do, you will be forced to

_____ in gym jail until you get _____ . The
     VERB   VERB (PAST TENSE)

game can get pretty _____ ! If you want my advice,
                          ADJECTIVE

_____ as fast as you can, get the other team's _____ ,
   VERB   PLURAL NOUN

and then _____ run back to your safe _____ . The
              ADVERB   NOUN

game ends when one team grabs all the other team's _____ ,
                                                   PLURAL NOUN

placing them _____ on their side of the court. Have fun,
                  ADVERB

and be _____ out there!
           ADJECTIVE

MAD LIBS® is fun to play with friends, but you can also play it by yourself! To begin with, DO NOT look at the story on the page below. Fill in the blanks on this page with the words called for. Then, using the words you have selected, fill in the blank spaces in the story.

Now you've created your own hilarious MAD LIBS® game!

FIRST DAY OF SCHOOL MENU

A PLACE _____

SOMETHING ALIVE _____

ADJECTIVE _____

PLURAL NOUN _____

COLOR _____

ANIMAL _____

PLURAL NOUN _____

TYPE OF LIQUID _____

TYPE OF FOOD _____

SOMETHING ALIVE _____

PLURAL NOUN _____

TYPE OF CONTAINER _____

PLURAL NOUN _____

NUMBER _____

NUMBER _____

ADJECTIVE _____

MAD LIBS®
FIRST DAY OF SCHOOL
MENU

Here's what's on the menu for the first day of school in (the)

_____:
<u>A PLACE</u>

- **Welcome Back Soup and Salad:** Fresh green _____
  <u>SOMETHING ALIVE</u>

  with _____ carrots, _____, a sprinkling of
  <u>ADJECTIVE</u>   <u>PLURAL NOUN</u>

  _____ cheese, and tangy _____ dressing.
  <u>COLOR</u>   <u>ANIMAL</u>

  Comes with hard-boiled _____ and chicken noodle
  <u>PLURAL NOUN</u>

  _____
  <u>TYPE OF LIQUID</u>

- **First Day Entrée:** Fried _____ on a wheat bun with
  <u>TYPE OF FOOD</u>

  _____ and a side of _____. Comes with
  <u>SOMETHING ALIVE</u>   <u>PLURAL NOUN</u>

  a/an _____ of fresh pineapple and _____
  <u>TYPE OF CONTAINER</u>   <u>PLURAL NOUN</u>

- **FDOS Snack:** Pizza with _____-percent-milk cheese and
  <u>NUMBER</u>

  _____-layer chocolate cake with _____-cream
  <u>NUMBER</u>   <u>ADJECTIVE</u>

  frosting for dessert

MAD LIBS® is fun to play with friends, but you can also play it by yourself! To begin with, DO NOT look at the story on the page below. Fill in the blanks on this page with the words called for. Then, using the words you have selected, fill in the blank spaces in the story.

Now you've created your own hilarious MAD LIBS® game!

RECESS!

PART OF THE BODY _____

VEHICLE _____

VERB _____

PLURAL NOUN _____

VERB ENDING IN "ING" _____

ANIMAL (PLURAL) _____

VERB _____

ANIMAL _____

COLOR _____

NUMBER _____

VERB _____

NOUN _____

ADJECTIVE _____

VERB _____

VERB _____

ADJECTIVE _____

VERB _____

MAD LIBS®

RECESS!

You know what puts a smile on my _____ on the first

PART OF THE BODY

day of school? Recess! After riding around on my _____

VEHICLE

all summer, it can be hard to _____ in a classroom

VERB

and concentrate on math, English, or the history of the United

_____. Fortunately, recess takes place outside unless it's

PLURAL NOUN

_____ cats and _____. I like to

VERB ENDING IN "ING"   ANIMAL (PLURAL)

_____ around with my friends and play _____ tag

VERB   ANIMAL

or a game of _____ Rover. Sometimes we play _____

COLOR   NUMBER

Square. One time, we played a game of Hide and _____ that

VERB

went on for the whole recess because no one could find me hiding

behind the _____! Whatever we do, it's a/an _____

NOUN   ADJECTIVE

time of day to unwind and just _____. I think the teachers

VERB

like to _____ during recess, too. For some reason, they need

VERB

a break after teaching a class full of _____ students. Maybe

ADJECTIVE

that's why they never want to play _____ ball with us?

VERB

MAD LIBS® is fun to play with friends, but you can also play it by yourself! To begin with, DO NOT look at the story on the page below. Fill in the blanks on this page with the words called for. Then, using the words you have selected, fill in the blank spaces in the story.

Now you've created your own hilarious MAD LIBS® game!

HOMEROOM BLUES

PLURAL NOUN _____

NUMBER _____

CELEBRITY _____

ADJECTIVE _____

NOUN _____

VERB ENDING IN "ING" _____

PART OF THE BODY _____

NOUN _____

ADJECTIVE _____

PLURAL NOUN _____

ADVERB _____

VERB ENDING IN "ING" _____

ADJECTIVE _____

SILLY WORD _____

ANIMAL (PLURAL) _____

NOUN _____

ADJECTIVE _____

VERB ENDING IN "ING" _____

MAD LIBS®

HOMEROOM BLUES

On the first day of school, we get assigned _____ in
                                              PLURAL NOUN

homeroom. The good news is I'm only _____ rows away from
                                        NUMBER

my best friend, _____ . The not-so-_____ news is
                  CELEBRITY   ADJECTIVE

that Donna "the _____" Watkinson sits behind me. She's
                    NOUN

always _____ her _____ or squirming
       VERB ENDING IN "ING"   PART OF THE BODY

in her _____ . It's so _____! Plus, she
           NOUN   ADJECTIVE

always borrows my _____ and never returns them. She
                     PLURAL NOUN

also talks really _____ when we're supposed to be
                      ADVERB

_____ . It's _____ to concentrate when she's
VERB ENDING IN "ING"   ADJECTIVE

going "blah-blah-_____" all the time. But at least my desk is
                   SILLY WORD

right by the window. When I need a break, I look outside at the little

_____ that land on the _____ right outside our
ANIMAL (PLURAL)   NOUN

classroom. They are so cute and so _____ . I could watch
                                       ADJECTIVE

them for hours. I wish one of those birds was _____
                                               VERB ENDING IN "ING"

behind me instead!

MAD LIBS® is fun to play with friends, but you can also play it by yourself! To begin with, DO NOT look at the story on the page below. Fill in the blanks on this page with the words called for. Then, using the words you have selected, fill in the blank spaces in the story.

Now you've created your own hilarious MAD LIBS® game!

LET'S DANCE!

VERB ENDING IN "ING" _____

ADVERB _____

A PLACE _____

VERB ENDING IN "ING" _____

VERB _____

PART OF THE BODY (PLURAL) _____

ADJECTIVE _____

ANIMAL _____

ADJECTIVE _____

TYPE OF EVENT _____

TYPE OF FOOD _____

NUMBER _____

COUNTRY _____

VERB ENDING IN "ING" _____

PART OF THE BODY _____

ADJECTIVE _____

VERB _____

NOUN _____

MAD LIBS

LET'S DANCE!

On the first day of school, I saw this poster _____ in
_____ VERB ENDING IN "ING"

the hall:

You are _____ invited to the Fall Costume Ball!
_____ ADVERB

Please join us in (the) _____ for a night of music, dance,
_____ A PLACE

and _____ . Don't forget to _____
_____ VERB ENDING IN "ING" _____ VERB

a costume. You can be anything—a ghost, a monster with huge

_____ , or a/an _____ _____!
PART OF THE BODY (PLURAL) _____ ADJECTIVE _____ ANIMAL

There will be _____ treats from our _____
_____ ADJECTIVE _____ TYPE OF EVENT

planning committee. All _____ cookies will cost
_____ TYPE OF FOOD

_____ dollars, and proceeds go toward our class trip to
_____ NUMBER

_____ this spring. Don't forget your _____
COUNTRY _____ VERB ENDING IN "ING"

shoes as there will be live _____ -tapping music. We'll also
_____ PART OF THE BODY

have _____ games and prizes! _____ with us for
_____ ADJECTIVE _____ VERB

a/an _____ to remember!
_____ NOUN

MAD LIBS® is fun to play with friends, but you can also play it by yourself! To begin with, DO NOT look at the story on the page below. Fill in the blanks on this page with the words called for. Then, using the words you have selected, fill in the blank spaces in the story.

Now you've created your own hilarious MAD LIBS® game!

A TRIP TO THE NURSE

PERSON IN ROOM _____

VERB _____

VERB ENDING IN "ING" _____

NOUN _____

EXCLAMATION _____

ADJECTIVE _____

PART OF THE BODY _____

A PLACE _____

VERB ENDING IN "ING" _____

PLURAL NOUN _____

ADJECTIVE _____

VERB (PAST TENSE) _____

VERB ENDING IN "ING" _____

ADJECTIVE _____

ADJECTIVE _____

MAD LIBS

A TRIP TO THE NURSE

Nurse: Hi, _____ . What seems to _____ the
PERSON IN ROOM   VERB

problem?

Kid: Well, we were _____ a game of dodgeball and
VERB ENDING IN "ING"

I got hit with a/an _____ .
NOUN

Nurse: _____ ! That sounds _____ . So, it's your
EXCLAMATION   ADJECTIVE

_____ that hurts?
PART OF THE BODY

Kid: No.

Nurse: Oh. Okay. So why are you here in my _____ ?
A PLACE

Kid: Well, I was just _____ in the cafeteria. I had
VERB ENDING IN "ING"

spaghetti and _____ .
PLURAL NOUN

Nurse: And did that make you feel _____ ?
ADJECTIVE

Kid: Nope.

Nurse: So, you didn't get _____ in gym. And you didn't
VERB (PAST TENSE)

get sick from _____ lunch. I'm a little _____ .
VERB ENDING IN "ING"   ADJECTIVE

Why are you here?

Kid: My mother always says it's better to be _____ than sorry!
ADJECTIVE

MAD LIBS® is fun to play with friends, but you can also play it by yourself! To begin with, DO NOT look at the story on the page below. Fill in the blanks on this page with the words called for. Then, using the words you have selected, fill in the blank spaces in the story.

Now you've created your own hilarious MAD LIBS® game!

FIRST DAY OF SCHOOL CHEER

ADJECTIVE _____

VERB _____

NOUN _____

SILLY WORD _____

VERB ENDING IN "ING" _____

ANIMAL (PLURAL) _____

COLOR _____

PLURAL NOUN _____

EXCLAMATION _____

ADJECTIVE _____

OCCUPATION (PLURAL) _____

SOMETHING ALIVE (PLURAL) _____

PERSON IN ROOM _____

SILLY WORD _____

NOUN _____

PART OF THE BODY _____

Hooray, hooray!

It's a/an _____ school day!
ADJECTIVE

There's a test to _____
VERB

and a/an _____ to play!
NOUN

_____ , woo-hoo!
SILLY WORD

I've got _____ to do
VERB ENDING IN "ING"

about plants, and _____ ,
ANIMAL (PLURAL)

and _____ _____ , too!
COLOR   PLURAL NOUN

_____ , yippee!
EXCLAMATION

School's the _____ place to be
ADJECTIVE

for _____ and _____
OCCUPATION (PLURAL)   SOMETHING ALIVE (PLURAL)

and _____ and me!
PERSON IN ROOM

Oh, _____ ! Oh, wow!
SILLY WORD

The _____ is ringing now!
NOUN

Time to fill my _____
PART OF THE BODY

with lots of . . . know-how!

MAD LIBS® is fun to play with friends, but you can also play it by yourself! To begin with, DO NOT look at the story on the page below. Fill in the blanks on this page with the words called for. Then, using the words you have selected, fill in the blank spaces in the story.

Now you've created your own hilarious MAD LIBS® game!

CLUBS

ADJECTIVE _____

VERB _____

PLURAL NOUN _____

VERB ENDING IN "ING" _____

NOUN _____

PART OF THE BODY _____

VERB _____

ADJECTIVE _____

PLURAL NOUN _____

NOUN _____

SILLY WORD _____

VERB _____

ADJECTIVE _____

VERB ENDING IN "ING" _____

NOUN _____

PLURAL NOUN _____

ADJECTIVE _____

MAD LIBS

CLUBS

There are so many _____ school clubs to join! Which will
                 ADJECTIVE

you _____?
    VERB

- **Drama Club:** This year's production will be *The Sound of*

   _____. If you like singing and _____,
     PLURAL NOUN   VERB ENDING IN "ING"

   this is the _____ for you.
             NOUN

- **Garden Club:** Like getting your _____ dirty? Does
                        PART OF THE BODY

   watching flowers _____ make you _____?
                VERB   ADJECTIVE

   Come plant some _____ with us and see what grows!
              PLURAL NOUN

- _____ **Squad:** Rah! Rah! _____! Do you have
   NOUN   SILLY WORD

   energy to spare? Do you _____ your school? Join us and
                       VERB

   get _____. Goooo team!
       ADJECTIVE

- **Robotics:** Interested in _____ robots? Strengthen
               VERB ENDING IN "ING"

   your _____-welding skills, install circuit _____,
        NOUN   PLURAL NOUN

   and build _____ friendships!
          ADJECTIVE

MAD LIBS® is fun to play with friends, but you can also play it by yourself! To begin with, DO NOT look at the story on the page below. Fill in the blanks on this page with the words called for. Then, using the words you have selected, fill in the blank spaces in the story.

Now you've created your own hilarious MAD LIBS® game!

FIRST DAY AT HOME

COUNTRY _____

VERB ENDING IN "ING" _____

SOMETHING ALIVE (PLURAL) _____

ADJECTIVE _____

NOUN _____

NOUN _____

VERB _____

ADJECTIVE _____

TYPE OF EVENT (PLURAL) _____

PLURAL NOUN _____

SILLY WORD _____

TYPE OF LIQUID _____

ADVERB _____

ADJECTIVE _____

NOUN _____

VERB ENDING IN "ING" _____

ADJECTIVE _____

NOUN _____

Many students all over _____ celebrate the first day
COUNTRY

of school in their very own _____ room! Lots of
VERB ENDING IN "ING"

_____ are homeschooled or study remotely using
SOMETHING ALIVE (PLURAL)

only a/an _____ -speed modem, a/an _____ -less
ADJECTIVE   NOUN

webcam, and their laptop _____ . They like to _____
NOUN   VERB

on the first day of school in many _____ ways. Some of these
ADJECTIVE

students throw virtual _____ by inviting their best
TYPE OF EVENT (PLURAL)

_____ to hang out on a video conferencing site like
PLURAL NOUN

_____ .com. Others use _____ -color paints
SILLY WORD   TYPE OF LIQUID

to express how excited they are by _____ painting a/an
ADVERB

_____ picture! And some prefer to show their enthusiasm by
ADJECTIVE

performing in a dance _____ and _____ it
NOUN   VERB ENDING IN "ING"

online. But, no matter how they choose to celebrate, one thing is

_____ . . . everyone likes to celebrate the first _____
ADJECTIVE   NOUN

of school!